Rabbi Sabato Morais

— Pioneer Sephardic Rabbi of Early American Judaism —

by Rabbi Dov Peretz Elkins

Winner of the National Jewish Book Award

Mazo Publishers

Rabbi Sabato Morais
Pioneer Sephardic Rabbi of Early American Judaism

ISBN 978-1-956381-429

Contact The Author
RabbiElkins@gmail.com

Mazo Publishers
Website: www.mazopublishers.com
Email: info@mazopublishers.com

Dedicated To All My Teachers At The
Jewish Theological Seminary Of America

Contents

The Author

Rabbi Dov Peretz Elkins is a nationally known lecturer, educator, workshop leader, author, and book critic. He is a popular speaker on the Jewish circuit.

Rabbi Elkins is a recipient of the National Jewish Book Award, and the author of over 60 books. His *Chicken Soup For The Jewish Soul* was on *The New York Times* bestseller list.

His most recent books are: *The Battle Between The Menorah And The Magen David; Rabbi Alexander Goode: The Rabbi and His Three Fellow Chaplains Who Went Down with the USAT Dorchester; The Founder of Hasidism: Wisdom and Tales of the Baal Shem Tov; Peter Bergson – The Jewish Lobbyist Who Advocated To Save Jews During the Holocaust; The Friendship That Shaped Jewish History; Bialik: Israel's National Poet; The Power of Human Speech; FATE; Jewish Ethical Wisdom From Pirkei Avot; To Climb*

The Rungs – Memoirs of a Rabbi; Jewish Stories from Heaven and Earth: Inspiring Tales to Nourish the Heart and Soul; Tales of the Righteous, Simple Actions for Jews to Help Green the Planet; Heart and Scroll: Inspiring Stories from the Masters; In the Spirit: Insights for Spiritual Renewal in the 21st Century; For Those Left Behind: A Jewish Anthology of Comfort and Healing and *A Treasury of Thoughts on Israel and Zionism.*

Among Rabbi Elkins' other books are *Rosh Hashanah Readings: Inspiration, Information and Contemplation, Yom Kippur Readings,* and *The Wisdom of Judaism: An Introduction to the Values of the Talmud.* See other books by Dov Peretz Elkins at www.jewishgrowth.org.

Rabbi Elkins served in several outstanding congregations in Rochester, NY, Cleveland, OH, and in Princeton, NJ, before retirement. He earned a doctorate in pastoral counseling in Rochester, NY.

Dr. Elkins lives in Jerusalem with his wife, Maxine (Miryam). They have six children and twelve grandchildren.

Preface

This brief biography of Sabato Morais is not meant to be complete and comprehensive. It is designed for teenagers and young families. It is designed to spread the legacy of Sabato Morais.

The bulk of the essay was written as an assignment for Professor Salo Baron when I was a rabbinical student at The Jewish Theological Seminary of America (1959-1964). There has been a great deal of research done of the life of Morais in the past sixty years, and I have attempted to fill in the gaps that existed in the original essay.

Most of the references were brought to my attention by two very distinguished authorities on the subject, Professor Jonathan Sarna and Professor Arthur Kiron. Both Professor Sarna and Professor Kiron were kind enough to read the entire manuscript, and made many important suggestions and corrections. Any errors in the final essay are totally my responsibility.

I am particularly pleased to bring this biography to the general English-speaking public since I am a graduate of the institution that was inspired by an original seminary brought into being by Sabato Morais.

I express my appreciation to my publisher, Chaim Mazo, who has brought to light many of my recent books. And special thanks to my loving wife, Miryam (Maxine) for her unfailing patience during the writing of all of my books.

Dov Peretz Elkins
Jerusalem, Erev Pesah 5783
The fifty-sixth anniversary of
the reunification of the holy city of Jerusalem
The seventy-fifth anniversary of the State of Israel

Background and Birth

The Medici family had transformed a fortified castle into a thriving commercial center, known as Leghorn (*Livorno* in Italian). Being located on the west coast of Italy, it was opened as a free port in 1590 by Ferdinand I, Grand Duke of Tuscany. To further stimulate its growth, this prince threw open its shores to all religious and political refugees in this same year. Shortly thereafter, a group of Conversos and exiles from the Iberian peninsula were welcomed there by the Medicis, and a notable Jewish community was created. The building of synagogues and schools was followed by the establishment of a Hebrew printing press in the mid-seventeenth century, and another in the beginning of the eighteenth century. Leghorn became such a

Ferdinand I
Grand Duke of Tuscany

Inside the 16th century Livorno synagogue, which was destroyed during the bombings of the Second World War.

Simhat Torah holiday celebration at the Livorno synagogue, painted by Solomon Hart in 1850.

thoroughly Jewish city that Christian visitors were forced to observe the Jewish Sabbath, not being able to transact any business on that day.

Among the early settlers of Leghorn were the Montefiore and Morais families. They, too, were active in the religious and cultural life of Leghorn.

The memorial plaque on the birthplace of Moses Montefiore.

Several generations later, one of the Italian Jews since Moshe Hayim Luzzatto, a prominent rabbi, kabbalist and philosopher, was born to Samuel and Bona Morais, the third of nine children, on April 13, 1823 (Iyar 2, 5583). His mother's maiden name was Wolf and was probably of German origin. From her, young Sabato inherited a love for Torah and things Jewish. From his paternal side he inherited a flair for political and social causes. His father and grandfather were both active participants in the patriotic Italian unification movements and were members of the Order of Freemasons. His father was even imprisoned on one occasion for his political "offenses."

This passion for human freedom that Sabato saw and felt in his home was not wasted on him. He continued to carry that torch during his lifetime wherever he went – London, Philadelphia, and elsewhere. It is one of the distinguishing characteristics of his long and creative life. The duty of one person to rescue his suffering neighbor was felt by Morais so strongly that it informed his every action. It knew no racial, national, or religious boundaries. Morais was a dedicated Jew, but also a worthy citizen of the universe, and neglected neither his own people, his own coreligionists, or anyone who beckoned at his door for succor. We shall look for this humane thread to wind itself into a major thread in the tapestry of his active years in Europe and America. His secular humanitarianism made Morais inevitably a better Jew, and his intense Jewish training further nurtured this love of humanity and sense of responsibility to serve.

Youth and Education

Another major factor in understanding Morais's later years in the rabbinate is his education. He was not a product of the Eastern European *heder*. Morais was the heir of the dignified Sephardic lineage. His father was Sephardic, his mother Ashkenazic, but he lived as a Sephardic Jew who pronounced Hebrew with a grace and musical harmony, for whom all of Hebrew literature was significant – *Aggadah* no less than *Halakhah*, the Bible even more than the Talmud, which he also revered.

When Sabato was fifteen years old, his beloved mother passed away. This was a crucial period for him. Until that sad event he had not made up his mind about his profession. Now, he knew that he must accede to his late mother's fervent prayer that he become a rabbi and serve one of the neighboring communities in Italy.

With the vigor that would characterize his whole mature life, he took up more assiduously the study of rabbinic literature with such masters as Rabbi Funaro and Curiat, and the Chief Rabbi of Leghorn, Ḥakham Abraham Baruch Piperno. He had private attention in these studies and wasted not a minute. He was, therefore, able to pursue secular studies while completing his requirements for the degrees of *Ḥazzan* and teacher (*Hatarat Hora'ah*) with *Ḥakham* Piperno. He was never ordained as a *ḥakham* himself, the Sephardic title for rabbi, and hence never called himself Rabbi, but rather *Ḥazzan*.

Morais was a lover of language and mastered several European and Semitic languages. His native tongue was, of course, Italian. He mastered the literature and belles-lettres of his country and, in addition, learned French and Spanish literature. His depth of knowledge in Semitic languages, Hebrew and Aramaic, came from Professor Salvatore De Benedetti of the University of Pisa.

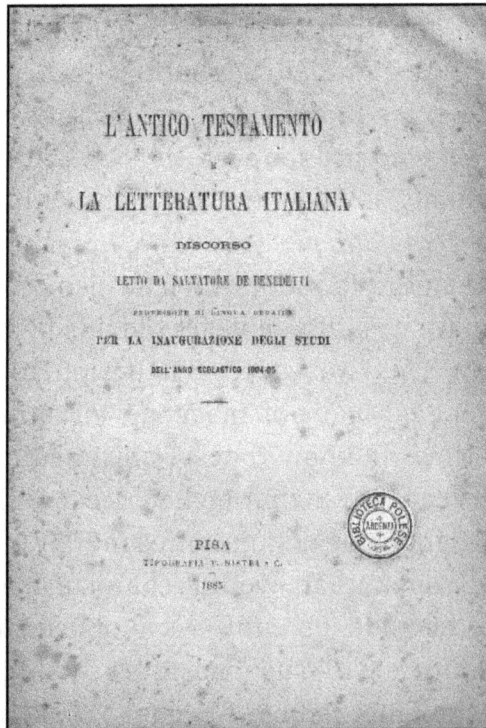

Pamphlet by Salvatore De Benedetti, 1867.

This interest in belletristic pursuits also became a distinguishing mark in the career of Morais. His facility in language enabled him to succeed as a writer and preacher when the need arose later on. We shall have more to say about this talent in our discussion of Morais the scholar.

It is ironic how the hand of God works in history sometimes. It is precisely because young Sabato could not speak English that he was rejected from a position in London that might have changed the course of his life. Had his interviewers any insight into the man, or lacking that, a prophetic ability to read some of the masterful English prose to flow from this gifted poet's ready pen later on, they would have sealed his fate for England and hence prevented him from taking up the cudgels of American Jewish leadership.

Transition Years: London

In 1846, Morais was already an ordained teacher, a scholar of note, and had acquired some beneficial experience in teaching young Italian children in his local community of Leghorn. All this at age 23. Therefore, when news came his way about an opening of the position of *Ḥazzan Sheni* (Assistant Cantor) at Kahal Kadosh Shaar Hashamayim at the Bevis Marks synagogue in London, a Spanish-Portuguese congregation, his initial reluctance to make the trip to apply was overcome by the persuasion of his close friends.

Because he did not speak English, Morais was rejected. It was a crushing defeat for him. A man of modest mien, his already weak sense of self-confidence must have been severely damaged. He made the weary trip back home to Leghorn and continued his studies and his teaching.

But Fate was on his side. He was to spend time in England, but not in a position enough to his liking for him to want to remain there. It would give him rich experience in an Anglo-Saxon milieu, vital for his future, but did not tie him emotionally or intellectually strongly enough to keep him there. Only a few months later he received

This photograph shows the Rev. Dr. David Aaron de Sola and his student and future son-in-law, the Rev. Abraham Pereira Mendes, standing in the Velho Sephardic Cemetery, Mile End, London. De Sola was ḥazzan of Bevis Marks Synagogue in London, circa 1848.

another offer, from the same congregation, to become Hebrew master in its Orphans School. He now left home for good. He spent five years in London, 1846–1851, and used these years to his distinct advantage. They would stand him in excellent stead for the great task awaiting him in the New World.

In London, Morais accomplished three things above all else: mastery of the English language, intense experience as an educator of young children, and an acquaintance with Joseph (Giuseppe) Mazzini, an outstanding figure of the Italian Risurgimento. At the Orphans School, Morais did such a capable job that his reputation as a teacher

This banner commemorates the founding of the Jews' Hospital in 1795 and the Jews' Orphan Asylum in 1831 in London. (jewishmuseum.org.uk)

who could inspire as well as inculcate reached the whole Jewish community there. His name passed by word of mouth among the leading Jews of London. The Montefiore family, also from Leghorn, asked him to come to their home and act as private tutor to their children. From that time on, he became close friends with Moses Montefiore.

Morais's family background and its reputation for intense participation in social movements were constantly with him. The Italian patriot and revolutionist Mazzini had been in Italy since 1837, working at revolutionary propaganda in an attempt to create a unified and free Italy. It was inevitable, even in metropolitan London, that he would meet Morais, son and grandson of Italian patriots. These two men became good friends and close associates. Mazzini had been fleeing from country to country in Europe to stir up Italian nationalism. He was an exile from his Mother Country. He called upon his intimate friend Morais to show his faith and trust in him in a tangible way. Mazzini needed a passport to transverse the capitals of Europe unnoticed, one that would not mark him by his family name, Mazzini. Morais thought Mazzini's work significant enough to take the risk and gave him his own passport to travel with. This is an interesting sidelight to Jewish history, one pointing up the strong nexus of liberal Jews with liberal movements of world history.

Joseph (Giuseppe) Mazzini

Mazzini had a profound influence on Morais's thinking and social technique, just as another patriot was to have on him later – Abraham Lincoln. It is interesting that these two non-Jewish patriots influencing Morais both had biblical names taken from the patriarchs of the Jewish religion.

The Mature Years: Arrival in America

In 1851, when Morais was 27 years of age, after having served in London for five years, he heard of a challenging offer from across the seas. Because of internal congregational politics, Isaac Leeser was compelled to resign his post as ḥazzan and preacher at the notable Sephardic synagogue in Philadelphia, Mikveh Israel. Again Morais was reluctant. It meant making a long journey to a foreign land. True, now he had overcome the one major obstacle that prevented him from being accepted at his first position in London; he now had competence in the English language. On the other hand, he had not yet conquered his diffidence in his own abilities. He, in fact, retained this sense of

Isaac Leeser

modesty throughout his life.

However, once again his friends prevailed upon him and he made the cumbersome trip to the shores of the New World. Morais appealed to the leaders of Congregation Mikveh Israel. Morais' humble appearance, his melodious voice, his experience in teaching, and his profound scholarship all ingratiated himself with the Board of Directors.

The Mikveh Israel Building in the time of Sabato Morais.

He arrived in New York on Friday, March 14, 1851, just before Purim, and began his service to Congregation Mikveh Israel on the Sabbath after Purim. Formal installation took place on April 13, 1851. Morais served that congregation in Philadelphia for 46 uninterrupted years as ḥazzan, preacher, and lecturer, until his death in 1897.

Four years after his arrival, Morais married a young woman of traditional Jewish upbringing, Clara Esther Weil, who died in 1872. Together they raised a large family of seven children and maintained a warm, traditional Jewish home, where Judaism was a blessing and created the loving atmosphere in which the children got a firsthand education in Jewish living. Their son Henry also entered the rabbinate and their daughter Nina chose the profession of a writer. They lived in a modest but comfortable home at 546 North Fifth Street, on the west side of the street, just below Green Street. This was very close to the location of Mikveh Israel's center city building in those years, on Seventh Street, north of Arch Street.

When Clara Morais died at age thirty-nine, their eldest daughter, Nina, who had just turned sixteen, took over many of the responsibilities of caring for the younger children and dealing with household chores. Her youngest brother was only two years old. Morais never remarried.

As Nina grew older, with fewer responsibilities, she become a teacher and then a superintendent at Philadelphia's Hebrew Sunday School. Eventually she became well-known as a writer and advocate for women's rights.

Congregation Mikveh Israel

The first problem Morais faced upon arrival in Philadelphia was the rift in Congregation Mikveh Israel between those who wanted to accept Ashkenazic Jews in their midst and those who violently reacted against the German Jews. This, and other issues, were strong enough of a problem for Leeser to have had to resign. It became more intense when Germans began pouring into America.

Morais was familiar with this smugness in England and knew how to fight it. And fight it he did, but tactfully and diplomatically. After almost two decades of battling, Morais won a life contract in 1868, indicating how well his mediation was accepted by all parties. In the interest of unity, Morais was willing to make many sacrifices, showing the qualities of a true diplomat and educator. A good teacher knows that he cannot fight equally as hard for every issue. For those things he deems vital, he must wage an all-out battle. For less important matters he must not yell too loudly, or people will stop listening. This quality of compromise made Morais the ideal leader of the community later in life, if we may foreshadow a bit. That is, compromise without sacrificing basic principles.

He was no ivory-tower leader, but a true teacher whose actions and thoughts were based upon full knowledge of his community.

For example, we may take the issue of liturgy. Morais was interested for many years in creating a unified ritual in the United States to eliminate confusion and redundancy. In a series of articles in *The Jewish Messenger* and *The Jewish Record of Philadelphia*, he proposed the convocation of a council to create a unified pattern for communal worship, which would result in organizing a standardized *siddur*. The amazing thing is that he suggested that this newly arranged *siddur* be based on the Ashkenazic ritual. As much as he loved the Sephardic version of the prayer service, he knew that compromise had to come first from himself. Unfortunately, his plans never materialized.

It is often said today that all rabbis are frustrated ḥazzanim, and all ḥazzanim are frustrated rabbis. Morais filled the roles of both ḥazzan and rabbi but was frustrated in neither. He had a beautiful voice and loved to lead the service and chant the prayers. Many of his melodious chants were brought by him from his native Italy. Morais' melodies for *Hallel* and *Adon Olam* were used long after his death, according to the late historian, Professor Moshe Davis. Once, on Yom Kippur, Morais chanted the entire service from start to finish, including blowing the shofar and preaching two sermons. This seems to have been his first love – leading the congregation in prayer.

As preacher, he was no less adept. He would write out each sermon with painstaking care, always quoting biblical and rabbinic sources wherever possible, and usually ended with a prayer that he composed, which would create a poetic and inspirational note to conclude his preaching.

Many of these he had printed in the various Jewish newspapers and journals of his day. Others still lay at first in manuscript form in the archives of Dropsie College. In 1986, Dropsie was reorganized as a post-graduate research center called the Annenberg Research Institute. In 1993, the Annenberg Institute (the word "Research" was dropped from the title) merged with Penn and was renamed the Center for Judaic Studies. In 1998, it was renamed the Center for Advanced Judaic Studies, and in 2008 it was endowed with a naming gift and renamed the Herbert D. Katz Center for Advanced Judaic Studies.

Herbert D. Katz Center for Advanced Judaic Studies in Philadelphia.

The Katz Center now houses his collection of papers and correspondence. His writings, sermons, and others touch on every conceivable subject; his interests knew no bounds. Anything that was Jewish was of profound concern to him. He published articles in such publications as *The Occident*, *The Asmonean*, *The Menorah Journal*, *The Jewish Record*, *The American Hebrew*, and *The Jewish Exponent*. They include topics "polemical, epistolary, homiletical, meditational, historical, theological and critical."

Of all his duties, the one that followed him throughout his life, in his native Leghorn, later in London, and finally in America, was that of an *educator*. A day did not go by in his life in which he did not in some way – personally, through correspondence, preaching or writing an article – to instruct his flock.

Morais was a born teacher. He had the instinctive feeling about getting his point across through education, and not through divine fiat, as it were. When he wanted to persuade his congregation that the sweeping reforms in ritual that were the order of the day were against the spirit of Jewish tradition, he said that he could merely have stated that he would not do it because it was written in his contract and in the constitution of the synagogue, that no such vast changes were to be made. "But I am anxious to reason with my brethren, to show cause for my opposition to changes in the service of the Synagogue."

In the education of the young in his congregation, he faced many of the problems that modern rabbis face today:

Answer, ye fathers and mothers in Israel. Of what does the religious education which you afford your children consist? Enlighten me, for I have in vain sought to discover it. Surely it is not in the mechanical repetition of a few blessings, the meaning of which they know not; nor is it in their instruction in a section of the Law when they reach the age of consideration.

Ironically, he quotes the answer of the parents:

Our daughter cannot appear to great advantage in society unless she understands the art of music and the exercise of dancing; our son cannot aspire to the name of learned, unless he is versed in Latin and Greek; but no one will ask them how far the knowledge of their religion extends – indeed, its study is quite superfluous, for time and age will teach it to them. Oh, how insane! We have sown in their hearts vanity and ambition, and can we expect that they will listen to the voice of pure religion, which is inimical to both?

About a century ahead of his contemporaries in the rabbinate, he early recognized that the educational program in an American synagogue must include the adults as well as the children. He had a thriving adult education program. He had classes going on every week in the synagogue building, until the snowball of his Adult Education Program turned into a national movement. As Dr. Moshe Davis points out, "Morais especially distinguished himself as a teacher of adults."

Morais' interest in Jewish education went beyond the walls of Mikveh Israel. He was a leader in the Hebrew Sunday School Movement in Philadelphia, where thousands of young children studied. He lectured on Jewish history at the YMHA (Young Men's Hebrew Association). His concern for the education of young Jews

The emblem of
The Hebrew Education Society in Philadelphia.

in his community is evidenced particularly strongly in a report he authored of the history and purposes of the Hebrew Education Society of Philadelphia. The fact that he wrote the report in Hebrew shows his concern for a living and dynamic process of ongoing creativity. It is interesting to point out in this connection that Morais was one of the few Jews of his day who could write the Hebrew language.

Following the example of his master, Ḥakham Piperno, Morais had a circle of students whom he trained personally in his own home. From that small circle emerged many great names in the annals of American Jewry, such as Cyrus Adler, Solomon Solis-Cohen, Mayer Sulzberger, Hyman Gratz, Moses Aaron Dropsie, Isaac Husik, and more. His home was a Bet Va'ad Leḥakhamim, and even on the day of his death he had students with him in his home.

Cyrus Adler   *Mayer Sulzberger*   *Moses Aaron Dropsie*

Champion of Human Rights

M orais's zeal for the amelioration of the lot of his fellow citizens has been traced, as we have seen, to his home, where his father and grandfather were members of the Freemasons. Sabato, too, as a young man in Italy, joined this organization. Even after his arrival to the shores of America, he maintained contact with Mazzini and spoke out for Italian unification: "Upon the soil of an independent and united Italy a mother's bosom shall not be rent; the young and innocent shall no more be robbed of their tutelary guardians."

Besides the influences of his home and that of Mazzini, a new influence came into the life of Sabato Morais in America, that of Abraham Lincoln. He respected Lincoln almost to the point of idolizing him. He was deeply shocked when the Great Liberator was assassinated.

Abraham Lincoln, 16th president of the United States.

Brethren! If the pulsations of my heart could assume human speech, they would best picture my mental agony upon that never-to-be-forgotten Sabbath. I had never concealed before my love for him who was chosen from among the lowly as a ruler over a great people. Yes, I loved every action, every word of that godly man. I loved him for his patriarchal simplicity. I loved him for his incorruptible character; I loved him for... his tender compassion for all the oppressed.

These were not idle words, if they were idolizing. Morais fought Lincoln's battle with him on his own home front every inch of the way. He even risked his job for its victory. In the very thick of the Civil War, he supported the Union (the Northern states of the United States, as opposed to the Confederacy, the Southern states, which wanted to withdraw from the Union). For this he was awarded an honorary membership in the Union League of Philadelphia.

At a very critical time during the war, the president of his congregation, Mr. Abraham Hart, sent a copy of his sermon and prayer to President Lincoln, who thanked him by letter.

But his congregation was less than happy with his preaching for Abolition. In 1864, special services were held on a national holiday, and in the sermon that day Morais referred

Abraham Hart

Home of the Union League of Philadelphia.

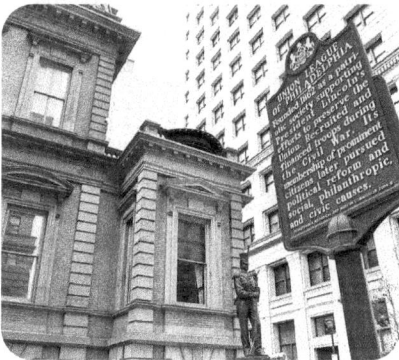

Union League of Philadelphia – Founded 1862 as a patriotic society supporting Abraham Lincoln's efforts to preserve the Union. Recruited and financed troops during the Civil War. Its membership of prominent citizens later pursued political reform and social, philanthropic, and civil causes.

to the State of Maryland, just free from slavery, as "Merry Land." In December of that year, the Board of Managers of the congregation adopted the following resolution:

"Resolved, that henceforth all English lectures or discourses be dispensed with, except by particular agreement of the Parnas [President] made in writing."

Morais was deeply disappointed, and some time later,

the following resolution was issued, slightly mitigating the dire effects on him of the first resolution:

"Resolved, that the Parnas be requested to direct the Reverend S. Morais to deliver a religious discourse on one Sabbath of each month, and any holiday."

By the following April 1865, when the war was over, further permission was granted to deliver lectures:
"upon moral and religious subjects only, on any day that the Synagogue shall be opened for Divine Services; and that on special occasions, whenever the Synagogue may be opened by order of the Parnas, he be permitted to speak on the subjects of the day."

After Lincoln was assassinated, Morais continued to fight for the dead leader's goals:
If his [Lincoln's] paternal voice could reach us from the seat of beatitude, it would exhort us to suffer further privations, to endure hardships, to bear even a temporary defeat, but never to pause until the flag of one reunited people shall wave from Maine to California, from the St. Lawrence to the Gulf of Mexico; for in that event not only our happiness and that of our children is involved, but the cause of human liberty is deeply concerned.

As soon as the restrictions placed upon him were loosened, his eloquent and fiery voice burst out once again for the cause of freedom and human liberty.
He clashed with his Board of Managers on other occasions as well, dealing with social and political issues.

"The Kidnapping of Edgardo Mortara",
painting by Moritz Daniel Oppenheim.

Another such instance is that of the famous Mortara case. A young Jewish lad of Bologna, Italy, was forcibly baptized and abducted, and the Church demanded that he receive a Catholic education.

A Jewish delegation to James Buchanan, the president of the United States, asked that he intercede with the Pope, but he would not. The following Sabbath, Morais refused to recite the prayer for the government. The action aroused the ire of the congregational board, and he was forced to recite it in following weeks.

The protection of the Labor Movement was not outside the purview of Morais's activities. In 1890, there was a strike in a garment factory, where the employers were Jews. On Yom Kippur of that year, Morais spoke out on the issue in his sermon, pleading with the management, in the spirit of the haftarah of that day:

"Do you fast for strife and contention? On the day of your fast you exact all your gains. Is not rather this the fast that the Lord hath proclaimed; that ye break the bonds of wickedness and let the oppressed go free? Visit the homes of your employees, see their misery and then make your amendment."

The strike was settled shortly thereafter.

After the May Laws of 1881 were enacted, Jews came swarming to America, and many of them to Philadelphia. Morais could not communicate with these people because he did not know Russian, German, or Yiddish, but he made contact in another way, even more important than in speech – he gave them his time and his energies in trying to help them adapt to their new life, to finding them jobs, and to supporting their initial adjustment period.

Morais's selfless contributions to all manner of philanthropic and educational causes never ceased. He fought for freedom wherever there was none, equality where it did not exist, and human rights where they were unknown. He helped Jew and non-Jew, white and dark, European and American. Both the poor and the needy benefited from him, the recent immigrant and the longtime resident who was momentarily stumbling.

One of the ways he created to channel charitable funds was established as a permanent institution in American Jewish life today. This is the Rabbi's Fund, which he initiated. He requested a sum of $300 from his congregation for "a special poor purse placed at the disposal of the Hazzan, to bestow as he may deem proper." According to Dr. Davis, this fund was used for "tools for gainful employment, good for trade, rented quarters for those who could not work because of the difficult winter, clothes for the children, medical attention for the ill."

Morais the Scholar

Morais was erudite in the highest literary sense of that word. His field was literature, as broad and as deep as that field can be. It encompassed the knowledge of several Indo-European and Semitic tongues and their literatures, and the ability to express himself in several of these languages. He achieved what most scholars long for in their esoteric pursuits, namely, the familiarity in depth with belles-lettres of all peoples and of all ages. Anything he learned, he learned well. In London, he was rejected for his lack of ability to handle English. After he studied that language and began to use it in speech and on paper, his excellence was quickly noticeable to any listener or reader. Witness the following passage from a sermon delivered on Thanksgiving day, chosen purely at random:

... the sweet breath of liberty does not extinguish the flame of religion ... Could religion be synonymous with servitude? Could religion thrive better in a soil bedewed with the tears of the oppressed than in a soil warmed by the sun of freedom?

In the foreword to a posthumous collection of his

writings on Italian Hebrew literature, Morais's son, Henry, writes that his father's scholarship was "vast and varied, embracing religion, theology, doctrines, politics, Hebrew literature, Jewish history (on which subjects alone, upwards of sixty lectures have been written, covering a period from Ezra and Nehemiah to considerably past the expulsion from Spain), articles and poems in the Hebrew language, in Italian... polemics, translations..."

Eliezer ben Yehudah arrived in Jerusalem in 1881, and he became the main driving force behind the revival of Hebrew as a modern, spoken language in Palestine. By 1922, enough Jewish pioneers were speaking Hebrew for the British Mandate authorities to recognize Hebrew as the official language of Jews in Palestine.

In two particular areas Morais seems to have excelled even more than others – the Hebrew language and biblical literature. He was one of the Jews in the world in the nineteenth century to actually precede Eliezer ben Yehudah in speaking Hebrew. In evaluating Morais's Hebrew poetry, Professor Moshe Davis admits that Morais's literary creations were not first rate, as poetry goes, but praises him as being one of the first to attempt writing Hebrew poetry in America.

His poems include tributes to Ḥakham Piperno, Solomon Rappaport, Moses Montefiore, Emma Lazarus, the Jewish congregation of Leghorn, B'nai B'rith. Davis also claims that Morais kept a daily diary in Hebrew, and he also wrote to pupils in Hebrew.

His great love for the Bible as the keystone of the Hebrew religion and culture was well known by all who knew him. The Chair in Biblical History and Literature at the Jewish Theological Seminary of America in New York was initially named after him since he was the first to hold it when the first Jewish Theological Seminary existed, simultaneously with his presidency. When, in 1923, Mikveh Israel arranged a memorial service to commemorate the 100th anniversary of Morais's birth, Solomon Solis-Cohen was one of the speakers:

"In all his teaching, public and private, he laid the greatest emphasis upon the Bible. Its text was at his instant command, and he was saturated with its spirit."

Solis-Cohen reports, too, that besides delving deeply into all of the traditional commentaries, Morais was equally conversant with the contributions of non-Jewish scholars of Bible and archaeology. This is obvious from the fact that he quotes non-Jews in his polemics against higher criticism. However, the very fact that he had read these modern works shows his understanding of the need to reckon with their contributions. He may have questioned their motives and many of their conclusions, particularly with regard to the Pentateuch, but he understood the necessity of knowing their works. He admitted that the text was not always perfect and that the chronologies did not always jibe. He acknowledged the necessity of studying the Greek and Aramaic translations of the Bible, Semitic languages, and Near Eastern archaeology.

His main interest in the Bible, however, was religious. He did not deny the charges of the higher critics because of their methods of arriving at them, but because of the lack of validity of their conclusions, which he found on objective grounds.

> ... those destined to ascend our pulpits shall draw knowledge at the fountain-head, not from streamlets running with corruption. The word of the Bible in its original purity shall command profound attention; its purport, when obscure, shall be sought at the hands of commentators, trustworthy by reason of their thorough acquaintance with the construction, the genius, the spirit of Holy Writ. Ewald shall not supersede our Kimchi and Nachmanides, nor shall Luzzatto be set aside to make room for Gesenius. Like the word of the Bible, so shall its history also be studied in the original, not in Kuenen, Wellhausen, or Robertson Smith; not in the works of Gentiles or Jews that deny Moses the authorship of the Pentateuch, make our patriarchs sheer myths, our priests tyrannical egotists, our Ezra a pretender, our progenitors unmitigated dupes.

And on another occasion, he said:

> The students shall study for a religious purpose, not archaeologically, to become ardent votaries to the service of Israel's God, not students of a chameleon-like philosophy, even changing with man's temper and surroundings.

Morais would have the curriculum of his Rabbinical School emphasize Bible over Talmud, and other worthwhile pursuits:

> As far as it lies in my power, the proposed seminary shall vindicate the right of the Hebrew Bible to a precedence over all theological studies. It

shall be the boast of that institute hereafter that the attendants are surpassing Scripturalists – if I may be permitted the expression – though they may not rank foremost among skilled Talmudists. The latter have, at times, degenerated into hair splitting disputants....

The 1917 translation of *The Holy Scripture* by the Jewish Publication Society contains Morais's translation of the Book of Jeremiah, which he prepared just before his death. His daughter, Nina, put the finishing touches on the unfinished translation.

Because of his depth and breadth of scholarship, his contributions to humanitarian causes, and his influence in the community of Philadelphia, Morais became the first Jew to be awarded the honorary degree of Doctor of Laws by the University of Pennsylvania. The degree was awarded on June 9, 1887.

Character and Appearance

Before we proceed with the events of a crowded and creative life, let us pause and describe Morais the man.

Our subject was a tall man with a dignified air about him. He looked the part of a scholar, his beard and deep-set serious eyes giving him a quality of saintliness that inspired reverence and respect. His pupil, William Rosenau, who also later became a scholar of note in his own right, recalls that Morais was 5'10" tall, having "silken hair with tender curls, deep-set dark eyes, a greyish beard, and possessed a sonorous, penetrating

Sabato Morais

but well-modulated voice. He was attired with high silk hat, black gown and talith whenever he performed the duties of reader and preacher."

If any one quality had to be singled out to describe him, it would certainly be that of deep and sincere humility. All of those relatives, students, and colleagues who have chosen to record their memories of him on paper seem to concur in emphasizing this one quality in all their descriptions of him.

At the 100th anniversary celebration of more Morais's birth, mentioned above, his son had this to say: "My father's main characteristic – modesty – that, too, which is a twin sister to learning."

The incumbent president of his congregation remembered him for his "true humility" which "was a pronounced feature of his career."

The first graduate of the Seminary, which Morais created, Joseph H. Hertz, later Chief Rabbi of the British Empire, wrote of his teacher, that "he had a selflessness, the moral strength, and saintliness, that the Prophets had – a mighty man, and yet one of the meekest of men."

Rabbi Dr. Joseph H. Hertz (1872-1946), who was elected Chief Rabbi of the British Empire in 1913.

Both times that opportunity knocked at his door, inviting him to apply for a position of importance – in London and in Philadelphia – Morais was reluctant to go because of his lack of confidence in his abilities. It was always his friends who had to persuade and cajole him into applying. Once, after he was already ḥazzan at Mikveh Israel, a leading rabbi in New York, Dr. Henry Pereira Mendes of Shearith Israel Congregation, recommended to his Board of Managers that they invite Morais to become their rabbi, and he, Mendes, step down to become his associate. Despite the increase in salary that this move would have meant to Morais, he declined the offer. Morais always referred to himself as "Mr." until the University of Pennsylvania conferred upon him the honorary degree of Doctor of Laws.

Morais was offered other such lucrative posts in New York, and another in England to replace the Chief Rabbi Benjamin Artom. He declined these, too.

Rabbi Benjamin Artom (1835-1879) became the Chief Rabbi of the Spanish and Portuguese congregations of the United Kingdom in 1866.

Once, when the congregation's funds were low, he voluntarily offered to take a substantial reduction in his salary. Of necessity, his offer was accepted, but his full salary was restored a few years later.

But we learn of Morais's personal humility not only from the tributes of others. His own writings drip with the sense of holiness of life and of man, which prevented him from becoming arrogant or haughty. At the celebration of the laying of the cornerstone of Mikveh Israel's new building, Morais told his congregation:

> My beloved hearers! Let us allow ourselves one moment's reflection ere we bury beneath yonder stone the memorials of our age; for, if there be pride in us, if the vanity of exhibiting a more sightly structure than others possess, impelled us to designate this place as our future synagogue; if a hankering after the acclamation of the world incited us to convene this vast multitude together; if temporal gain or the ambition of a name was our stimulus in cooperating to speed this holy task, let us then bury first such unholy feelings in the bosom of the earth.

Leader of the Historical School

The nineteenth century saw the growth of two major movements in Judaism, both originating in Germany. The first was Reform, a radical reaction away from traditional Judaism, denying major Jewish principles such as circumcision, *kashruth*, the traditional Sabbath observance, Hebrew, the centrality of Eretz Israel, etc. The reaction to this was what was known as the Historical School – the movement desiring to retain the main elements of historic Judaism while making changes to meet the needs of the times, just as Judaism had always done historically.

There developed among German Jewry a "Science of Judaism," represented mainly by Leopold Zunz, a new method of studying Jewish history. The method was to look objectively at the history of Jewish Law and practice, and literature. The results of this method were the conclusions that Jewish religion had never remained static.

There were constant changes throughout history, to meet the needs of the times. The Historical School meant merely to bring Judaism up to date once again, as it had done in the past. To its leaders, it was certainly the

Leopold Zunz

mainstream of Jewish life and thought. It was no departure from the past, merely a continuation of it, a logical and historical continuation of it, true to its character of constant development.

With the transfer of Reform to America, the same challenge brought itself to the fore and the same reaction set it. Another Historical School developed to combat the growth of Reform once again. Morais was not one of the leaders of the American continuation of the Historical School. His background was Sephardic, as pointed out earlier, not a congealed Eastern European one.

One of the particularly sensitive areas of disagreement between the Reformers and the Historical School was changing the prayer book. The Reformers had made vast omissions and alterations. Morais's own words can best summarize his position:

> The demand is for a simpler prayer book, and
> to effectually stop capricious changes, it must

unavoidably be granted. Expunge, then, what relates to the ordinances followed by the ancients in the performances of sacrificial rites; strike out what belongs to Mishnaic and Talmudic lore; reduce the number of Psalms now to be daily rehearsed; avoid, as far as practicable, the reiterating of supplication, confession, or sacred song; eschew the utterance of all sorts of denunciations; compare philologically long-established Rituals; study to discover in them what is more correct in diction, select what is more chaste in style, more exalting in ideas and what is more likely to have emanated from the venerable body whose leading spirit was, our second Moses, even, Ezra the priest. Then endeavor to fill up a portion of the empty space made empty by our expurgatory process with compositions suited to our existing wants. The printed and inedited writings of our philosophers and poets can supply a vast deal; the learning of our modern Rabbis may also be of service in that department...

Whatever ritual is agreed upon for the Jews of the United States of America must be in the language the house of Israel have ever used in communing with God: The Hebrew Language.

... joint singing should constitute the main part of the religious exercises... A judicious selection from our Psalter, interspersed with the best Hebrew hymns from ancient and modern poets; the rehearsing of the benedictions preceding and succeeding the "Shema"... the "Shemone Esre"... the perusal of the Law in a tricnnial cycle, if it is universally adopted by the Hebrew community in the United States.

Morais wrote often of his love of his Sephardic background:

"I grew in the love of the observance of Judaism in the fond attachment for the Sephardic Minhag, the only ritual existing in my native city. The very melodies, especially those of the New Year and the Day of Atonement had a charm which the softest of musical strains cannot surpass."

In an open letter to Kaufmann Kohler, a leader of Reform, Morais spelled out the philosophy of the Judaism which he espoused:

Not every custom to which your unsophisticated fathers adhered, flowed from a high source. Those who are conservative because they recognize in "orthodoxy" the depository of eternal principles, do not claim for each Jewish practice a Divine origin and immutability; but neither do they cast aside olden ritualism without the certainty that its absence can be supplied by what exceeds it in fitness and sterling worth.

At any event, we of the present century absolutely need a code where the rules which an American Israelite has ritually to follow on all occasions through life, are laid down unequivocally, with clearness and brevity, and likewise with due regard to our changed condition.

The position of Morais was that we are willing to examine our tradition carefully in the light of the best objective scholarship, but not to butcher it recklessly by throwing out the baby with the bathwater, to mix a metaphor. We are willing to make changes, and then, having made them, draw up an organized code pointing out the changes and the remaining obligations, but we must do it with greater care than the Reformers have, with more of a wholesome respect for the tradition.

Morais proposed to have changes in tradition made not by individuals at their own instincts, but by an organized "synod" of scholars who would decide jointly and make one uniform ritual:

> If changes are needed; if a modified ritual Code is demanded by the times, the subject would... be discussed with uniformity of purpose, and all the combined learning required would be brought to bear on the solution of a question vitally important to Judaism.

Until such time as a synod could meet and propose changes, Morais would maintain the ritual as is. But, he would begin to teach people the prayers, thus, in his own words:

> Instead of reforming religion, let us reform education. Meanwhile to familiarize with the prayers the attendants of this Synagogue, and also to secure more harmony in our popular chanting, I will devote one evening each week to the rehearsal of the same.

In other words, as Davis puts it, "Morais placed the program of the School in proper focus by seeking the reforming of Jews rather than the reform of Judaism."

Despite his ideological disputes, many of them fierce in intensity, catching up in their clutches the whole community of American Jewry, Morais never ceased to maintain cordial relations with all Jews on a personal level. He never fought with people, he fought against ideas in favor of other ideas that seemed to him more favorable and acceptable.

When a Reform congregation in Philadelphia, Keneseth Israel, celebrated the 70th birthday of its rabbi, Samuel Hirsch, a bitter ideological opponent of Morais, the latter attended the party in Dr. Hirsch's home.

When a memorial service was held for Adolph Cremieux, an intercongregational service at the Reform congregation Rodef Shalom on Broad Street, all of the rabbis in Philadelphia argued over what to wear. Each insisted on donning his own costume – cap, gown, talit, etc. Morais suggested that they follow the practice of the host congregation, Rodef Shalom, and all wear Prince Albert coats and hats.

Morais mourned the death of Isaac M. Wise, founder of American Reform, with Reform leaders of the community. And when Morais himself passed on, he was eulogized by the convention of Reform rabbis in Atlantic City, New Jersey.

I think it can be said, hopefully, in honesty and accuracy, that it is because of the pattern of gentlemanly and mature behavior of Sabato Morais that to this day his successors are on such good personal terms with leaders of other movements. There exist no bitter feelings between most Orthodox, Conservative, and Reform leaders. There is mutual respect and a clear understanding of their similarities and differences, which in no way affect personal relationships. This is indeed a great legacy.

There had been several attempts previously to establish a school in the United States for the training of rabbis and teachers. The first experiment was undertaken by Isaac Leeser. It was founded in Philadelphia on July 1, 1867,

Isaac Mayer Wise

and took the name of Maimonides College, after the great medieval scholar, rabbi, teacher, legalist, philosopher, and physician – the symbol of what the school might aim at producing. But when Leeser died, the school died with him, only six years after its birth. Morais had given it his full support and served as Professor of Biblical Exegesis during its short lifespan. The school had been the first operational rabbinical seminary in the Western world.

Two years later, Isaac Mayer Wise opened another rabbinical school, this time in Cincinnati (1875), the Hebrew Union College. Morais was in favor of any move to strengthen American Judaism, and so he put his weight behind this venture as well. He reasoned that this school

Isaac Leeser
(1806-1868)
Marker in Philadelphia: The eminent Jewish leader is buried here. Minister, Congregation Mikveh Israel, 1829-1850. Founder of the influential journal, The Occident, 1840; its publisher until 1868. A teacher and scholar, he translated the Hebrew Bible into English, 1853.

should be an academic institution with freedom of interpretation and could therefore train Reform rabbis as well as traditional spiritual leaders. He accepted the position of Examiner of the new college and remained in that part-time capacity for a decade.

The major break came when the Reform Movement served a "trefa banquet," and came out with their celebrated Pittsburgh Platform in 1885, named for the place of their convention that year. In it they declared that such major and fundamental Jewish principles as *kashruth*, circumcision, the traditional observance of the Sabbath and festivals, etc. were no longer relevant, and need not be observed. This was going too far. The movements began to close ranks, the lines of difference hardened.

Morais, discouraged by the abortive attempt to found a rabbinical college in Philadelphia, nevertheless saw the need for a school now to train traditional rabbis who would stem the tide of Reform. Perhaps in New York, the new center of American Judaism, he would have more success. In any case, the attempt had to be made. The character of American Judaism was at stake, and perhaps even its very existence.

He began to rally support among members of the Historical School, Benjamin Szold in Baltimore, H.P.

Mendes in New York. He began to build his "bulwark of defense to our belief" at the age of 63. He called it his Benjamin, the child of his old age.

Only two years after the announcement of Reform's Pittsburgh Platform, on January 2, 1887, Morais presided over the formal opening of The Jewish Theological Seminary Association, a name chosen by Alexander Kohut, overruling Morais's own suggestion of "The Orthodox Seminary." Classes were held at first in the vestry of Shearith Israel synagogue in New York City, and later at Cooper Union. Morais's energy and commitment to the education of the young is manifest in the fact that he helped establish the Seminary in his sixties. Already in declining health, he established and administered the Seminary, and traveled to New York City on a regular basis.

The preamble to the Seminary's constitution and by-laws reflects the feelings in the minds of the founding fathers:

> The necessity having been made manifest for associated and organized effort on the part of the Jews of America faithful to Mosaic Law and ancestral traditions, for the purpose of keeping alive the true Judaic spirit; in particular by the establishment of a Seminary where the Bible shall be impartially taught, and the Rabbinical literature faithfully expounded, and more especially where youths desirous of entering the ministry may be thoroughly grounded in Jewish knowledge and inspired by the precept and the example of their instructors with the love of the Hebrew language and a spirit of fidelity and dedication to the Jewish Law; the Subscribers have, in accordance with a resolution adopted at a meeting

of ministers held Shebat 25, 5646 (January 31st, 1886) at the Synagogue Shearith Israel, New York, agreed to organize The Jewish Theological Seminary Association.

From the inception of The Jewish Theological Seminary Association and until his death, a span of over a decade, Morais served as founding president of the Jewish Theological Seminary and also taught classes as its Professor of Bible. He made frequent visits to New York, often in times of "severe bodily suffering" and immense physical strain.

The new seminary saw some hard years in that decade, but with the spirit of Morais behind it, it could not stumble. However, after his death in November 1897, there was fear that it, too, might go the way of Maimonides College after Leeser's death. To prevent this from happening, Solomon Schechter was called from England to reorganize the Seminary and breathe new life into its bones. He arrived in 1902. At that point, the Jewish Theological Seminary, started by Sabato Morais, ceased to exist, and a new institution, called the Jewish Theological Seminary of America (JTSA) was established. While some scholars consider Morais as the Founder of the modern Conservative movement, among more recent scholarship, it is felt that the movement really began with the arrival of Solomon Schechter.

The first Jewish Theological Seminary placed its emphasis on study of Bible, more than Talmud, and on personal moral qualities – especially humility. The Jewish Theological Seminary of America (JTSA) began in 1902 with the arrival of Solomon Schechter (1847-1915),

The discovery by Solomon Schechter, the American Judaic scholar and educator, of a fragment of the Hebrew text of Ecclesiastes attracted world-wide attention to the famous Cairo Geniza. Subsequently, he rescued rare Hebrew religious manuscripts and medieval Jewish texts from the Genizah and brought them to Cambridge University.

placed emphasis on Wissenschaft des Judentums (Science of Judaism), the application of the new methods of textual study, especially philology and history, to the study of *Jewish* texts and the history of Judaism.

In the twentieth and twenty-first centuries, there has never been any doubt that the new Seminary has been a permanent star in the galaxy of Jewish religion and culture. It has created a dynamic, meaningful movement, which in the early decades of the twenty-first century encompasses over 550 Conservative congregations and over 1700 rabbis in the Rabbinical Assembly, mostly trained by its faculty.

While some consider Morais to be the founder of the Conservative Movement, in thought and practice, he considered himself Orthodox. For the record, it is unusual for a Sephardic rabbi to be called "Orthodox" or "Conservative." These movement appellations generally apply to Ashkenazic Jews and Jewish institutions. So whether Sabato Morais was the founder of "Conservative Judaism," as some claim, is a moot question. He was neither Conservative or Orthodox. He was Sephardic.

Death

Morais died on November 11, 1897, at the age of seventy-four, in the city where he spent the majority of his life – Philadelphia. He had been ill some time before dying, but never ceased teaching, preaching, and educating American Jewry. Even at his last moment, he was engaged in teaching one of his favorite pupils the desserts of Hebraic scholarship – medieval Hebrew poetry. Death came after three quarters of a century of creative contribution to Jewish life in Europe and America.

His funeral was attended by thousands, including many immigrant Eastern European Jews who lost a day's pay to attend that rainy day. Historians note that his funeral was the first such mass funeral among Jews in America – unprecedented in American Jewish history.

In an Orthodox newspaper Morais was mourned as "without doubt ... the greatest of all orthodox rabbis in the United States. The New York Times obituary remembered him as a "powerful and aggressive factor in discussions of vast import and interest to millions of people; a deep, incisive, fearless thinker, speaker, and writer." One scholar described him as "not only one of the most beloved of

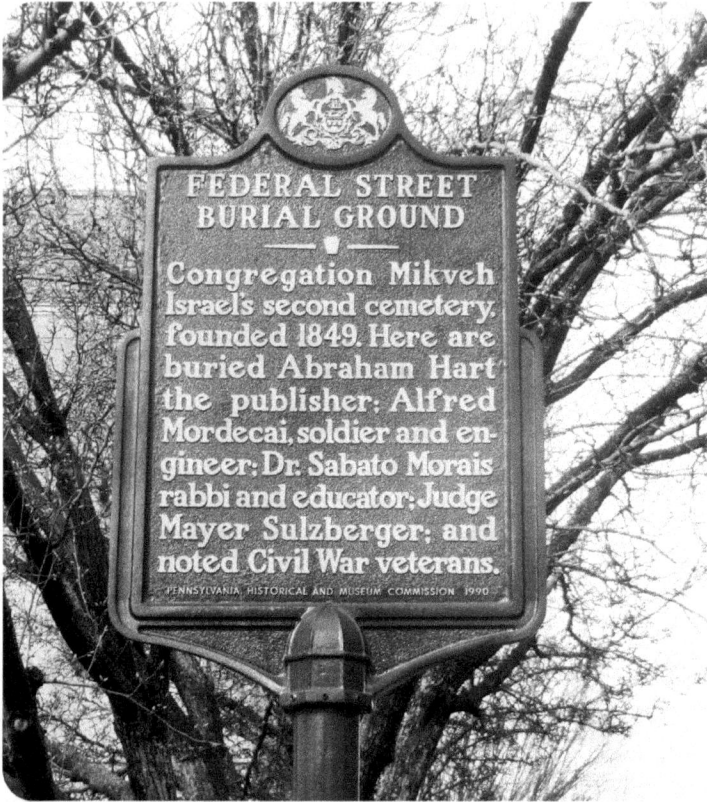

The Pennsylvania Historical & Museum Commission erected this historical marker at the Federal Street cemetery in Philadelphia in 1990, marking that Rabbi Sabato Morais and other Jewish notables are buried there. This cemetery belongs to Congregation Mikveh Israel, Philadelphia's oldest synagogue.

local American Jewish leaders, but a political activist and cultural force whose concerns were national and international in scope."

In his modesty, Morais had stipulated that no eulogy be delivered over his remains and no special memorial service. Nevertheless, he was mourned by thousands in America and all over the world. Huge crowds thronged as they carried his remains through the streets of his adopted city. He was mourned by members of every faction in the Jewish community, colleagues, students, friends, congregants, and people who had only read his articles or heard his name.

Great tributes were paid to his memory by the secular and religious press. The world, and particularly the Jews, knew that they had lost a giant from their midst, an exceptional leader, one who had taught and fought for his ideals and convictions all his life, one who had created a school to train rabbis and teachers, which was followed by a new and stronger Seminary, and an ideal that lives today in the character of the American Jewish community.

Bibliography

Adler, Cyrus. "Sabato Morais, Founder of the Seminary," in *Mikveh Israel: Commemoration of the One Hundredth Anniversary of the Birth of Sabato Morais* (Philadelphia: Congregation Mikveh Israel, 1924).

Central Conference of American Rabbis, *Yearbook* 9 (1898).

Cohen, Charles J. "Doctor Morais's Relationship to the Congregation," in *Mikveh Israel: Commemoration of the One Hundredth Anniversary of the Birth of Sabato Morais.* (Philadelphia: Congregation Mikveh Israel, 1924), 7–16.

Columbia Encyclopedia. s.v. "Mazzini, Giuseppe," "Leghorn" (2nd ed.; New York: Columbia University Press, 1956).

Davis, Moshe. "Sabato Morais: A Selected and Annotated Bibliography of His Writings," *Publications of the American Jewish Historical Society* 37 (1924): 55–93.

———. "Shabtai Morais: Toledotav, Dayotav, U-feulotav" ("Sabato Morais: His Life, Thought, and Activities") in *Sefer Hashanah leYehudei America (The American Hebrew Yearbook)*, VII, ed. Menahem Ribalow (New York: Histadruth Ivrith of America, 1944), 574–92. Hebrew.

———. *Yahadut America Behitpathutah (The Shaping of American Judaism)* (New York: Jewish Theological Seminary of America, 1951). Hebrew.

————. *The Emergence of Conservative Judaism: The Historical School in 19th Century America* (Philadelphia: Jewish Publication Society of America, 1963).

Drachman, Bernard. "Sabato Morais: A Tribute," in *Mikveh Israel: Commemoration of the One Hundredth Anniversary of the Birth of Sabato Morais* (Philadelphia: Congregation Mikveh Israel, 1924), 49–53.

Elmaleh, Leon H. "Tribute," in *Mikveh Israel: Commemoration of the One Hundredth Anniversary of the Birth of Sabato Morais* (Philadelphia: Congregation Mikveh Israel, 1924), 56–61.

Glenn, Menahem G. "Rabbi Sabato Morais' Report on the Hebrew Education Society of Philadelphia," in *Essays in American Jewish History: To Commemorate the Tenth Anniversary of the Founding of the American Jewish Archives*, ed. Jacob Rader Marcus (Cincinnati: American Jewish Archives, 1958), 407–24.

Goldman Alex J., "Sabato Morais: Pillar of Strength and Determination," in *Giants of Faith: Great American Rabbis* (NY: Citadel Press, 1964, pages 99-114).

Hertz, Joseph H. "Sabato Morais: A Pupil's Tribute," in *The Jewish Theological Seminary of America Semi-Centennial Volume*, ed. Cyrus Adler (New York: Jewish Theological Seminary of America, 1939), 5-6, 46-48.

Karp, Abraham J. "The Origins of Conservative Judaism," *Conservative Judaism,* 19.4 (1965).

Kiron, Arthur, "Heralds of Duty: The Sephardic Italian Jewish Theological Seminary of Sabato Morais." Jewish Quarterly Review, Vol. 105, No. 2 (Spring 2015) 206–249.

————. "Dust and Ashes: The Funeral and Forgetting of Sabato Morais." American Jewish History, Vol. 84, No. 3 (September, 1996), pp. 155-188.

Kiron, Arthur. "Golden Ages, Promised Lands: The Victorian Rabbinic Humanism of Sabato Morais" (Ph.D. diss., Columbia University, 1999.

Morais, Henry S. *Eminent Israelites of the Nineteenth Century: A Series of Biographical Sketches* (Philadelphia: Edward Stern and Company, 1880).

———. *The Jews of Philadelphia: Their History from the Earliest Settlements to the Present Time* (Philadelphia: Levytype, 1894).

———. "Unveiling the Tablet," in *Mikveh Israel: Commemoration of the One Hundredth Anniversary of the Birth of Sabato Morais* (Philadelphia: Congregation Mikveh Israel, 1924), 43-45.

———. "Foreword," in Sabato Morais, *Italian Hebrew Literature*, ed. Julius Greenstone (New York: Jewish Theological Seminary, 1926).

Morais, Sabato. *A Sermon Delivered on Thanksgiving Day (November 25, 1852): Before the Congregation Mikve Israel* (Philadelphia: n.p., 1853).

———. *Report of the Committee of Arrangement for Laying the Corner Stone of the New Synagogue of the Portuguese Congregation "Mickve Israel"* (Philadelphia: Collins, 1859).

———. *An Address on the Death of Abraham Lincoln* (Philadelphia: Collins, 1865).

———. "Mickve Israel Congregation of Philadelphia," *Publications of the American Jewish Historical Society* 1 (1893): 13–24.

———. *Italian Hebrew Literature*, ed. Julius Greenstone (New York: Jewish Theological Seminary, 1926).

———. "The Death of Abraham Lincoln," in *Abraham Lincoln: The Tribute of the Synagogue*, ed. Emanuel Hertz (New York: Bloch, 1927).

———. "A Discourse (June 1, 1865)," in *Abraham Lincoln: The Tribute of the Synagogue*, ed. Emanuel Hertz (New York: Bloch, 1927), 9ff.

———. "Can We Change the Ritual?" in *Tradition and Change: The Development of Conservative Judaism*, ed. Mordecai Waxman (New York: Burning Bush, 1958).

———. "A Jewish Theological Seminary," in *Tradition and Change*, ed. Mordecai Waxman (New York: Burning Bush, 1958), 157-61.

Nadell, Pamela S. "Defender of Her Sex and Her People: Nina Morais Cohen," in *Yearning to Breathe Free: Jews in Gilded Age America*, eds. Adam D. Mendelsohn and Jonathan D. Sarna (Princeton: Princeton University Press, 2022).

Nathan, Marvin. "Discussion," *Yearbook of the Central Conference of American Rabbis* 33 (1923): 370-74.

Rosenau, William. "Sabato Morais: An Appreciation on the Centenary of His Birth," *Yearbook of the Central Conference of American Rabbis* 33 (1923): 356-70.

Sarna, Jonathan. *JPS: The Americanization of Jewish Culture.* (Philadelphia Jewish Publication Society, 1989).

Sarna, Jonathan. *American Judaism: A History*. Second Edition. (New Haven: Yale University Press, 2019.

Sarna, Jonathan, and Benjamin Shapell. *Lincoln and the Jews: A History*. (New York: Thomas Dunne Books, 2015).

Simonhoff, Harry. *Saga of American Jewry, 1865-1914* (New York: Arco, 1959).

Solis-Cohen, Solomon. "Sabato Morais: Necrology," *Publications of the American Jewish Historical Society* 8 (1900): 149-52.

———. "Sabato Morais, Teacher and Leader," in *Mikveh Israel: Commemoration of the One Hundredth Anniversary of the Birth of Sabato Morais* (Philadelphia: Congregation Mikveh Israel, 1924), 19-30.

Waxman, Mordecai (ed.). *Tradition and Change* (New York: Burning Bush, 1958).

Images
Wiki Commons
———. Fifty Years of Work, Hebrew Education Society of Philadelphia.

www.ingramcontent.com/pod-product-compliance
Lightning Source LLC
Chambersburg PA
CBHW070027110426
42741CB00034B/2670